SALLY FORTH®

by Greg Howard

D1007609

FAWCETT COLUMBINE • NEW YORK

A Fawcett Columbine Book
Published by Ballantine Books

Library of Congress Catalog Card Number: 86-92120

ISBN: 0-449-90260-9

Manufactured in the United States of America

First Edition: September 1987

10 9 8 7 6 5 4 3 2 1

SALLY'S HINTS FOR THOSE TRYING TO DO IT ALL

(1) DON'T SLEEP.   Incredible as it may sound, some people waste as much as 8 or 9 hours a day sleeping. One can achieve a 50% increase in productivity merely by ceasing this slothful habit.

(2) DON'T EAT MEALS.   If you really must eat, do so only on the run. It's good for your figure and saves needless wear and tear on chairs.

(3) DON'T CLEAN.   There is a fixed amount of dirt in this world. "Cleaning" consists largely of moving said dirt from one place to another. I, for one, find such behavior silly except when my mother is coming to visit.

(4) USE SPARE TIME WISELY.   The foregoing hints should give you several hours of spare time a week. You might want to consider using them to violate hint (1).

1-2
howard

1-3
howard

1-4
howard

1-13

DID I HEAR YOU RIGHT? YOU WANT ME TO SKIP MY POKER GAME FRIDAY SO WE CAN GO OUT TO DINNER?

RIGHT.

BUT IT'S MY NIGHT WITH THE BOYS. WE DRINK BEER, SMOKE CIGARS, TELL RAUNCHY JOKES, EXAGGERATE PAST ATHLETIC TRIUMPHS, BOAST OF BUSINESS CONQUESTS, AND BLUFF EACH OTHER OUT OF MONEY.

I PLAY POKER FOR **YOU**, SAL, SO THOSE URGES DON'T BUILD UP TO TOXIC LEVELS... IT'S SORT OF A MACHO RELEASE VALVE.

HAVE YOU DONE A VALENTINE FOR EVERYONE IN YOUR CLASS?

EXCEPT TOMMY JERKFACE... HE HIT ME TODAY.

HIS NAME ISN'T "JERKFACE," HILARY. AND YOU CAN'T LEAVE HIM OUT OR HE'LL FEEL BAD. PICK ONE FOR TOMMY.

OKAY, BUT I'M DOING THIS UNDER PROTEST.

2-13

HOW ABOUT THIS ONE? "ROSES ARE RED, VIOLETS ARE BLUE; MY MOTHER MADE ME SEND THIS TO YOU."

howard

4-26

24

5-19

howard

WHAT ARE YOU DOING, TED?

I'M FIXING STROGAN-OFF, RICE, TOMATOES VINAIGRETTE... OH, AND APPLE PIE FOR DESSERT.

howard

I LEFT WORK EARLY AND ON THE WAY HOME DECIDED THAT YOU DESERVE TO HAVE SOMEONE COOK A FANCY DINNER FOR YOU. SO I STOPPED AT THE SUPERMARKET AND THEN CAME HOME TO COOK MY LITTLE FINGERS OFF.

5-20

WHY IS IT I HAVE THE FEELING ROD SERLING IS GOING TO STEP IN AND WELCOME ME TO "THE TWILIGHT ZONE"?

CARE FOR AN ONION CANAPÉ?

LOOK, SAL, I REALLY DO WANT TO BEGIN TRYING TO SHARE MY FEELINGS WITH YOU, BUT I'VE GOT TO CRAWL BEFORE I CAN WALK.

I UNDERSTAND, TED.

I MEAN I CAN'T JUST SPILL MY GUTS THE FIRST DAY... I CAN'T JUST BLURT OUT "I L-O-V-E YOU" RIGHT AWAY.

"L-O-V-E"?

CAN WE START WITH SOMETHING LIKE "I ENJOY YOUR COMPANY"?

2-8

36

7-9

38

7-13

8-11
howard

koward 8-16

44

IS MOM UP YET?

SHE'S IN A VERTICAL POSITION IN FRONT OF HER CLOSET.

THAT'S NOT "UP." "UP" IS WHEN SHE'S ABLE TO WALK AND UTTER A VAGUELY COHERENT THOUGHT.

CHOOSE YOUR WEAPON, FUNNY MAN. I GET THE SHAVING CREAM.

SHE'S UP, DAD.

8-23 howard

55

UH, OH... WHERE'S THE SMILING FACE THAT GREETS ME EVERY MORNING?

DROWNING IN A SEA OF SELF-PITY.

WHAT'S WRONG?

THE GUY I'VE BEEN DATING FOR THREE MONTHS GOT ENGAGED TO HIS FORMER GIRLFRIEND, I LOST A FAMILY RING MY MOM GAVE ME, MY BIKE GOT STOLEN...

I BROKE MY LITTLE TOE WHEN I FELL DOWN THE STAIRS, MY RENT WENT UP EIGHTY BUCKS A MONTH, I'M COMING DOWN WITH THE FLU...

HERE'S YOUR LUNCH, HILARY.

NOT THE LUNCHBOX, MOM! I'VE GOT TO HAVE A BROWN BAG.

BEFORE SCHOOL STARTED YOU TOLD ME YOU ABSOLUTELY **HAD** TO HAVE THIS PARTICULAR LUNCHBOX. WE DROVE TO EVERY STORE IN TOWN BEFORE WE FOUND ONE, AND IT COST $8.95. NOW YOU TELL ME YOU WANT A BROWN BAG?

WHAT HAPPENED?

PEER PRESSURE CLAIMED ANOTHER VICTIM.

11-21

Howard

THE EXECUTIVE COMMITTEE LAUGHED AT MY IDEA ABOUT VACATION PAY THIS MORNING AND IT'S YOUR FAULT.

MY FAULT?

HAVE YOU FORGOTTEN THE CLAUSE IN YOUR JOB DESCRIPTION THAT SAYS YOU'RE SUPPOSED TO PREVENT YOUR BOSS FROM EMBARRASSING HIMSELF WITH STUPID IDEAS? YOU FAILED TO DO THAT, SALLY...

12-4

AND THAT'S THE REASON I TOLD THE EXECUTIVE COMMITTEE THE VACATION PAY IDEA WAS REALLY YOURS.

RALPH...

OKAY, MAYBE YOU'RE RIGHT, TED. MAYBE I HAVE A FEW UN-DESIRABLE "TYPE A" PERSONALITY TRAITS.

I'M CONCERNED THAT STRESS MAY AFFECT YOUR HEALTH, SAL.

12-19

WHAT AM I SUPPOSED TO DO ABOUT IT?

THIS ARTICLE SAYS "START BY TAKING STOCK OF WHAT IS REALLY IM-PORTANT TO YOU."

STOCK? GOOD GRIEF! I FORGOT TO GIVE RALPH THE ANSWER TO A STOCK OPTION QUESTION HE ASKED ME TODAY. MAYBE I CAN REACH HIM AT HOME.

howard

1-5

howard

11-5

WELL, I SUPPOSE I BETTER GET IT OVER WITH.

I'M A BRIGHT PERSON... I'VE GOT A RESPONSIBLE JOB... I MAKE COUNT-LESS DECISIONS EVERY DAY...

3-2

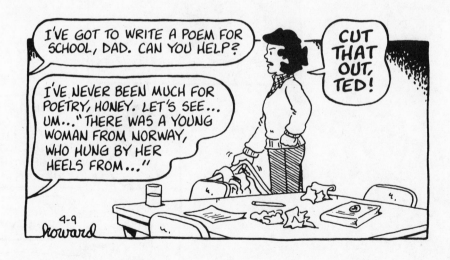

WELL, HOW DID YOUR TEACHER LIKE YOUR POEM?

SHE THOUGHT IT WAS GREAT EXCEPT FOR ONE STANZA.

WHICH ONE?

THE THIRD ONE. SHE SAID IT WAS STIFF AND LACKED YOUTHFUL EXUBERANCE.

4-12

HEY, THAT'S THE PART I HELPED WITH!

MY TEACHER SAYS SHE CAN SPOT PARENTAL POETRY WITH HER EYES CLOSED.

100

5-2

107

SEE, I TOLD YOU... I LOOK JUST FINE IN MY SWIMMING TRUNKS.

HOW IS IT THAT MEN STAND IN FRONT OF MIRRORS AND DON'T SEE THE FAT THEY HAVE WHILE WOMEN STAND IN FRONT OF MIRRORS AND SEE FAT THEY **DON'T** HAVE?

5-8

IT'S A GIFT.

THAT'S WHAT YOU CAN GIVE ME ON MY NEXT BIRTHDAY.

111

115

SO YOU WANT AN IM-PRESSIVE HAND-SHAKE? I CAN SHOW YOU A TRICK.

OKAY.

IT'S CALLED THE "PREMATURE SQUEEZE TECHNIQUE"... LOTS OF GUYS USE IT. YOU JUST START SQUEEZING BEFORE THE OTHER PERSON'S HAND IS ALL THE WAY IN YOURS. YOU CAN CRUNCH HIS FINGERS WITHOUT MUCH EFFORT AT ALL.

5-21

IT MAKES THE OTHER GUY FEEL LIKE A REAL WIMP.

DO YOU HAVE PERMIS-SION FROM THE OLD-BOY-NET-WORK TO SHOW ME THIS?

howard

117

5-26

6-16

ALL I WANTED TO BUY WAS A PLAIN OLD PAIR OF SNEAKERS, TED.

BUT THE SHOE BUSINESS HAS BEEN TAKEN OVER BY BLATANT MARKETING GIMMICKS. DO YOU REALIZE SHOES HAVE **NAMES** THESE DAYS? "PEGASUS," "HURRICANE," "MOTIVATOR"... REEBOK EVEN HAS A SHOE CALLED THE "CHARISMA." CAN YOU IMAGINE? "CHARISMA"?

6-18

WHAT COLOR DID YOU GET IT IN?

"MIAMI VICE PINK."

5-25

In October, 1978 Greg Howard was a partner in a large Minneapolis law firm and was incapable of drawing a stick-person without tracing. Although attempting to becoming a syndicated cartoonist was not, perhaps, a very logical career move at that point in his life, he left his law practice to pursue that goal. In May of 1980, after spending a year and a half trying to force himself to acquire a modicum of drawing ability and other skills necessary to develop a successful comic strip, "Sally Forth" was born. "Sally" was syndicated in 1981 and now appears daily on the comics pages of over 200 newspapers.

Howard and his wife have three teenagers and make their home in Minneapolis.